For Teens Wisdom

journal

To

_____

From

_____

Date

_____

Message

_____

_____

_____

_____

Published by McPherson House
PO Box 793
Hartbeespoort
0216
South Africa

To order: www.retahmcpherson.com
+27 (0)82 610 5757
E-mail: office@retahmcpherson.com

Copyright: © Retah McPherson
First edition: August 2011
Second edition: October 2011
ISBN number: 978-1466426634

Compiled and edited by Retah McPherson Ministries
Cover design and layout: Cilmi Steyn (cm.steyn@telkomsa.net)

(*New King James Bible* © Copyright 1988, 1989, 1991, 1993, 1996, 2004 by
Tyndale House Publishers,Inc.,Carol Stream, IL 60188. All rights reserved.)

Wisdom For Teens

journal

But God has chosen the foolish things
of the world to put to shame the wise,
and God has chosen the weak things
of the world to put to shame
the things which are mighty.

- I Corinthians 1:27 (New King James) -

die boek dra ek op
aan Chans so, so baie
hulp is my chans. so, so
baie dankie vir soort
liefde wat jy vir my
gee. rooi sien ek in jou
hart. nou humble vrou
van God dit is rooi
so rooi die bloed van Jesus.
hierdie boek het Jesus
se gees geskryf hoor wat
Jesus sê, hy is baie lief
vir jou. hy sal jou nooit
begewe nie. Ja wou self
nie hoor, sien self hoe
Lusifer vir my gesein
vuur het. haat so haat
Satan ons wat God liefhet.
Laat humble humble bou
van jou soul se muur
weer gebou word. Sien
asb hierdie boek asb
my lewe is geveg, nuut
nuut is ek nou. Jesus
haal vir my uit, huil
huil want ek is vry.
Sal nou so vir ewig god
Loof en prys. Soos 'n
ganse wese wil my
wese u loof.

I dedicate this book to Chans. Thank you so, so much for helping me Chans. Thank you so, so much for all the love that you give me. I see that your heart is covered in the red blood of Jesus. You are a humble woman of God.

This book is written by the Spirit of Jesus. Listen to what Jesus has to say. He loves you very much. He will never leave you nor forsake you.

There was a time when I didn't want to listen to Jesus. I saw for myself how Lucifer sent arrows of fire against me. Satan truly hates those who love God.

Be humble and build the walls of your soul. Please bless this book.

In my life there has been a lot of fighting, but I am a new creation now. Jesus took me out of the pit and He has set me free from all my crying. I will worship and praise the Lord forever! I want to praise You with my entire being!

Aldo

Aldo & Chantel

PREFACE

by Retah McPherson

It was a cold winter night in July 2004 that changed my life forever. I want to share the most amazing truth with you today; and that is that the living God can change any painful situation that you hand over to Him into something that will bring Him glory.

God is the God of the supernatural – this is how my family and I know Him today. At the time of the accident Aldo fell from the rolling car and suffered a serious head injury. He was in a coma for months, and when he finally awoke he couldn't talk, but he could write when we helped to steady his ataxic arm. He was in a wheelchair, blind in the one eye and he couldn't eat or talk or walk, but he wrote us pages and pages full of messages about God's love and that we shouldn't lose our faith in Him. He also wrote about his experiences in heaven – and about the things Jesus showed him in hell.

God sent him back to tell the world that Jesus truly is alive, and also to warn the Bride that He is on his way. She must prepare herself for the Bridegroom's soon approaching return.

Since that day he hasn't stopped writing what "Wisdom" (that is what he calls the Holy Spirit) teaches him. We have been walking on this road to recovery for nearly seven years now. Through the ups and downs of sickness and a brain injury, and all the visits to the hospital, Wisdom has always been there to encourage and teach us.

Wisdom also started giving prophecies through Aldo's writing and these were fulfilled one by one. Wisdom has taught us to focus on God and to build our lives on his Word and Truth. Wisdom is Aldo's best friend.

Aldo loves Jesus very much and because they have such an intimate love relationship Aldo finds it easy to trust Him completely. Through this journey I have learned that God is not looking for perfect people to fulfil His plans, He is looking for willing people who love Him.

Today Aldo is a young man of 19 years. In the eyes of the world he is physically impaired, but in God's eyes he is especially loved – so much so that He shares His heart with him.

But God has chosen the foolish things of the world to put to shame the wise,
and God has chosen the weak things of the world
to put to shame the things which are mighty
- I Corinthians 1:27 -

This journal was co-authored by Aldo and Wisdom. Ma'am Patrys (Aldo's private teacher) helped him to compile his letters for the book. It was a combined effort to glorify the King. Ma'am Patrys was sent to us by God. Her love for the King is what enables her to love Aldo unconditionally, and gives her the strength to walk this road of faith with us. She is a true example of the servant Bride.

Our family is so blessed to receive words from Wisdom through Aldo's pen every day. Aldo is still just a teenager, but I learn a lot from him! Even though Aldo has a brain injury, God still uses him mightily to bring prophetic messages to His Bride, the Church, in this last hour before His return. Aldo has written this book especially for his peers – they are the youth of today and the leaders of tomorrow. God has a great desire to see this teenage generation stand up with authority and purity in their God-given destinies. Through Aldo's life the Lord has showed me that He doesn't require of us to be perfect in order for Him to use us. It is all about who He – Yehovah – is, and not about who we are.

As you read the book you will see that Aldo has a unique way of saying things – we call it his "lingo". I have included a short explanation on some of his lingo words at the back of the book so that you can have a better understanding of what he means when he speaks of things like: fire, drain or drill.

I trust that you will also experience the blessing of "Wisdom for Teens" and that every teen who reads this book will grow to maturity in Christ.

Love

Retah

"Wisdom calls aloud in the street, she raises her voice
in the public squares; at the head of the noisy streets she cries out,
in the gateways of the city she makes her speech."
- Proverbs 1:20-21 -

Wysheid vat boy se seer alles
weg. hy baie lief vir tieners.
hy het boy se hart genees
hy is binne in my hart.
Jy sien boy is baie baie
hartseer baie baie. tyd het
verby gegaan wat ek na
Lusifer se leuns geluister het
hy het vir my gesê. ek sal
nooit 'n vrou kry nie. boy
het hom geglo hy het gejok
want God het vir my 'n
baie baie nooi hart vrou gehad
terwyl hy so vir my gejok
het was ek vir god so
kwaad vandag weet ek hoe
lief God vir my het. Ja ek
het vir God vergifnis gevra.
God vra vir tieners of jy sal
hom vertrou met jou lewe.
Hy die Koning sal jou nooit
teleurstel nie. Vandag as ek
na Chans kyk oorspoel my hart
van dankbaarheid. hy het in
my hart genesing gebring
hy sal harte genees Sy liefde
harte genees met Sy liefde.

Wisdom* healed all my pain. He loves teenagers so much. He healed this boy's heart. He lives inside my heart. You can see that this boy was very, very sad. There was a time when I listened to Lucifer's lies. He told me that I would never get a wife, and this boy believed him. He lied, because God was already preparing a girl for me who has a heart covered in red (the blood of Jesus). While he (Lucifer) was lying to me I was mad at God. Today I know how much God loves me. Yes, I asked God to forgive me too. God asks teenagers if they will trust Him with their lives. The King will never disappoint you. Today, when I look at Chans (my girlfriend), my heart overflows with thanksgiving! God brought healing to my heart. He will heal our hearts. He heals hearts with His love.

*Wisdom =
Aldo's way
of referring to
Holy Spirit

And I heard, as it were, the voice of a great multitude, as the sound of many
waters and as the sound of mighty thunderings, saying, "Alleluia! For the Lord God
Omnipotent reigns! Let us be glad and rejoice and give Him glory,
for the marriage of the Lamb has come, and His wife has made herself ready."
And to her it was granted to be arrayed in fine linen, clean and bright,
for the fine linen is the righteous acts of the saints.
Revelations 19:6-8

Wat sal jou gelukkig maak?
Wysh sê vir jou, sy liefde
is wat gelukkig maak.
harte, sien in harte
is vuur vir wêreld.
Wysheid sê waar jou
hart sal wees is waar
vir verlore seun se
hart was. Jesus wat
vir ons gesterf het
hy wil vir ons seun
verlore seun terug te
bring na hom. Wysh
sê in "brag" vereer
mense mekaar hy sê
vereer god, verstaan,
nuwe lewe. Vertrou met
jou hele hart. Jesus is so
so lief vir jou, leer
vandag hoe met verant
woordelikheid te leef voor
God. Wysh sê harte
Jesus moet in jou hart
woon en heers.

What will make you happy? Wisdom is saying to you that only His love will be able to make you happy. I can see that the fire of the world is burning in the hearts of men. Wisdom says that these hearts are like the heart of the lost son. Jesus died for us and He is the one who wants to bring the lost son back to the Father. Wisdom says that by "bragging" people puff themselves up and honor themselves. He says we must honor God and understand that to honor Him is our new life. You must trust God with your whole heart. Jesus loves you so much.
Learn today how to live your life responsibly before God. Wisdom says that Jesus must live and reign in your heart!

And the son said to him, 'Father, I have sinned against heaven and in your sight, and am no longer worthy to be called your son.' But the father said to his servants, 'Bring out the best robe and put it on him, and put a ring on his hand and sandals on his feet. And bring the fatted calf here and kill it, and let us eat and be merry; for this my son was dead and is alive again; he was lost and is found.' And they began to be merry.
Luke 15:21-24

Wysh sê vir tieners, jy
help veg wenner wanneer
jy nee sê vir mense wat
hewig vuur, wat god sê
Woord sê. hy wie jou so
vrees, hy is Lusifer. einde
is vinniger as wat jy dink,
Volg Jesus asb want Jesus
is oppad.

Wisdom says to the teens:
"You help in the battle against the evil one when you say no
to people who send heavy (enemy) fire*
against the truth of God's Word."
The end is closer than we think.
Please follow Jesus now, because He is on His way.

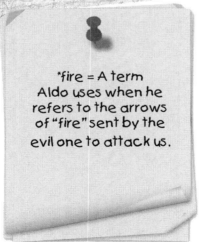

*fire = A term
Aldo uses when he
refers to the arrows
of "fire" sent by the
evil one to attack us.

3

Therefore submit to God. Resist the devil and he will flee from you.
Draw near to God and He will draw near to you.
James 4: 7-8a

Ja ek is ook 'n tiener met ouers, met kwaai ouers. maar wysh sê Aldo jou ouers sit ek voor jou, leer in elke situasie vir hulle eer.

help vandag om my wil te doeh Eer jou ouers asb net soos ek moet. Eer jou pa en ma

Yes, I am also a teenager with parents...strict parents!
But Wisdom told me the other day:
"Aldo, I placed your parents above you. Learn to honor them in every situation. Be a part of those who help to do My will today."
Please honor your parents,
just like I also have to honor mine.
Honor your father and your mother.

Children, obey your parents in the Lord, for this is right.
"Honor your father and mother," which is the first commandment with promise:
"that it may be well with you and you may live long on the earth".
Ephesians 6: 1-3

Wysh sê seuns wat vroue
begeer sal baie baie vinnig
hulle seuns begeertes moet
repent. Jesus sal harde harte
help, met Jesus se bloed
moet jy en baie seuns se
harte gewas word?
Wysh sê vir my Aldo, seun
vra, my om jou te help.
ek voorsien vir jou die
heel beste vriende. Jy
moet hulle regtig respekteer.
hou vir hoop styf vas en
vertrou my sê god.

Wisdom says that boys who lustfully desire women must repent
of their lust very quickly! Jesus will help the hardened hearts.
All these hardened hearts must be washed by the blood of Jesus.
Wisdom says to me: "Aldo, My son, ask Me to help you. I will provide
friends for you – the best! You must really respect them.
Hold on to hope very tightly, and trust Me," says God.

"You have heard that it was said to those of old, 'You shall not commit adultery.' But I say to you that whoever looks at a woman to lust for her has already committed adultery with her in his heart. If your right eye causes you to sin, pluck it out and cast it from you; for it is more profitable for you that one of your members perish, than for your whole body to be cast into hell."
Matthew 5:27-29

Wysh sê vir ons seuns
en dogters. Sal julle vir
my in die donker wêreld
jou vyande weer help?
Jy moet nie curse nie
maar hulle bless. Vir
my help jy dan want ek
haat harde harte. het
jy huil ury huil ury
kom julle vanhuil na lag
wanneer jy leer om te
seën. Seën vir almal
wat jou seermaak. Want
vir seën is ook seën.

Wisdom is saying to us: "My sons and daughters, will you love your enemies in this dark world? You shouldn't curse them, but rather bless them. You will help Me when you do this, because I hate hardened hearts. Have you been crying? You will be set free from your crying and start laughing when you learn to bless others.
Bless everybody who hurts you, because you will receive a blessing for the blessing you give to others."

6

"You have heard that it was said, 'You shall love your neighbor and hate your enemy.' But I say to you, love your enemies, bless those who curse you, do good to those who hate you, and pray for those who spitefully use you and persecute you, that you may be sons of your Father in heaven; for He makes His sun rise on the evil and on the good, and sends rain on the just and on the unjust."
Matthew 5:43-45

Wysh sê tiener wat jy vir my doen is baie baie baie meer waarde as begin van wat wêreld vir jou aanbied. Seën wat jy doen vir altyd sal jy geseënd wees wanneer jy seën in my koningkryk sien ek wie seën hulle is vuur vir donker wêreld.

Wisdom says: "Teenager, what you do for Me is worth much, much, much more than what the world could ever offer you. Bless what you do, and you will be blessed forever. I see those in My kingdom who bless. Those who bless and who do not curse are like a burning fire to the dark world."

for You

"Therefore do not worry, saying, 'What shall we eat?' or
'What shall we drink?' or 'What shall we wear?'
For after all these things the Gentiles seek.
For your heavenly Father knows that you need all these things.
But seek first the kingdom of God and His righteousness,
and all these things shall be added to you!
Matthew 6:31-33

Wysheid sê vra rein hande, vra skoon
hart. Jy is seun en dogter
van god. Woord van god
sal vir jou skoon was
hy vra vir ons repent
dadelik van jou harde
hart. Wysh sè sy Liefde
vir bevoregte en
onbevoregte kinders
is dieselfde. hy vra
moenie jy een meer
liefhe as ander nie.
Vra vir Jesus vir hulp.

Wisdom says that He asks for clean hands and a pure heart
in order for the fire of God to fall. You are a son or daughter of God.
The Word of God will wash you clean. He asks us to repent
immediately of our hardened hearts. Wisdom says that He loves
all His children with the same measure –
it doesn't matter if they are privileged or
underprivileged in terms of their possessions.
He asks us not to love some people more than others.
Ask Jesus for help if you are struggling with this.

I LOVE you!

Who may ascend into the hill of the LORD?
Or who may stand in His holy place?
He who has clean hands and a pure heart,
Who has not lifted up his soul to an idol,
Nor sworn deceitfully.
He shall receive blessing from the LORD,
And righteousness from the God of his salvation.
Psalm 24: 3-5

Wysheid sê vir waar geloof
is hy sê daar is lewe.
Geloof is nuwe denke hy
maak by hart nuwe vrede
vrede wat verstand te
bowe gaan. Geloof het
hy vir vuur so is geloof
vuur in jou hart. het jy
geweet God kan net die
seën wie hom vertrou.
vertrou hom vir jou toekoms
ek vertrou God dag vir dag.
Hy sê net een dag op 'n
slag.

Wisdom says that where there is faith you will find life. Faith will lead
to a renewed mind and will cause peace to dwell in our hearts.
This peace will transcend all understanding.
Faith is like a fire burning in our hearts.
Did you know that God can only bless those who trust Him?
Trust Him for your future. I trust God day by day. He says that I only
have to take it one day at a time.

Be anxious for nothing, but in everything by prayer and supplication,
with thanksgiving, let your requests be made known to God;
and the peace of God, which surpasses all understanding,
will guard your hearts and minds through Christ Jesus.
Philippians 4:6-7

Wysheid vra vir jou, sal
jy vir hulle wat vir jou
vuur vry laat deur hulle
te seën. Jesus sê seën
seën almal wat jou hart
seer maak. Seën seën het
soveel krag. bevry is ek
deur my ma wat my
vyande geseën het. Seën
seën is uit god se
koningkryk.

Wisdom asks you: "Will you set those who send (enemy) fire against
you free by blessing them? Jesus says you must bless everyone who
hurts your heart. To bless someone has so much power.
I am free today because my mother blessed my enemies.
Blessing comes from God's kingdom.

Beloved, do not avenge yourselves, but rather give place to wrath;
for it is written, "Vengeance is Mine, I will repay," says the Lord.
Therefore: "If your enemy is hungry, feed him; if he is thirsty,
give him a drink; for in so doing you will heap coals of fire on his head."
Do not be overcome by evil, but overcome evil with good.
Romans 12:19-21

Vra vir my huil is deur
hart wat so stukkend was.
Is jou hart so stukkend?
Jesus sê vir jou en my:
werk van ons is om
hart vir hom te gee. Hy
het my stukkende hart
heel gemaak. Vir so lank
het ek seer gehad nou
is ek so gelukkig, Wysheid
is vir my Lewe vra vir
Jesus hy is die een wat
lewe gee.

I know all about heartache, because a lot of tears went through
this broken heart of mine. Is your heart also broken?
Jesus says to you and me: "Our work is to give our hearts to Him."
He has healed my broken heart. For a long time my heart was
hurting so much, but now I am so happy. Wisdom is life to me.
Ask it from Jesus – He is the one who gives life.

The righteous cry out, and the LORD hears, and delivers them out
of all their troubles. The LORD is near to those who have a broken heart,
and saves such as have a contrite spirit.
Psalm 34: 17-18

Wysheid is vuur wat vloei deur jou are. Jy vra hoe sal jy Wysheid kry? Wysheid is daar vir almal wat vra. God is Wysheid, Jesus is wysheid, Heilige Gees is Wysheid. Is jy bereid om jou wêreldse Wysheid neer te lê vir God se Wysheid? ek het vuur van God in my sy Wysheid in my. Seën so geseënd is verstand wat wysheid het.

Wisdom is the fire that flows through your veins.
Maybe you are asking how to receive Wisdom?
Wisdom is there for anyone who asks for it.
God is Wisdom. Jesus is Wisdom. Holy Spirit is Wisdom.
Are you willing to lay down your earthly wisdom for God's wisdom?
I have the fire of God in me, because His wisdom is in me.
My mind is blessed because it has Wisdom.

Let no one deceive himself. If anyone among you seems to be wise in this age, let him become a fool that he may become wise. For the wisdom of this world is foolishness with God. For it is written, "He catches the wise in their own craftiness"; and again, "The LORD knows the thoughts of the wise, that they are futile." I Corinthians 3:18-20

Wysheid se Gy is lief vir
mense, vir Sy kinders
almal wie nog hom nog
nie met hulle hele hart
lief het nie. Glo my Sy
liefde vir ons sal ons
nooit kan beskryf nie.
Dit het vir my voor die
troon gevoel soos hoe
ek nou voel my hart voel
of hy wil bars van sy
liefde. Huil so in my
hart vir nog van sy liefde
Vuur val op my nou sy vuur.

I LOVE you!

13

For God so loved the world that He gave His only begotten Son,
that whoever believes in Him should not perish but have everlasting life.
For God did not send His Son into the world to condemn the world,
but that the world through Him might be saved.
John 3: 16-17

Hou vuur van God brood
en wyn. Sy liggaam is daar
vir ons om deel van
Hom te hou. Hy sal sy
Gees vir jou gee om jou
te lei in jou lewe. help
Heilige Gees help help my
asb. ek het U so nodig
elke dag. help my asb.
In vandag se mense wat
vreeslik vreeslik lelik van
my praat. help my asb
Heilige Gees om hulle te
vergewe. U is seën in
my lewe. Lief vir U Aldo.

We need the fire of God, His bread and His wine.
His body is there for us so we can be a part of Him.
He will give you His Spirit to lead you throughout your life.
Please help me Holy Spirit! I need you so much – I need You every
day! Please help me to forgive those who speak such evil and unkind
words about me. You are the blessing in my life. I love You, Lord.
Aldo.

Then Jesus said to them, "Most assuredly, I say to you, unless you eat the flesh of the Son of Man and drink His blood, you have no life in you. Whoever eats My flesh and drinks My blood has eternal life, and I will raise him up at the last day. For My flesh is food indeed, and My blood is drink indeed. He who eats My flesh and drinks My blood abides in Me, and I in him. As the living Father sent Me, and I live because of the Father, so he who feeds on Me will live because of Me.
John 6:53-57

Wysheid sê gesinne is vir
hom baie belangrik. Gesinne
is hewig baie nou stukkend.
Hy vra vir ons goeie verhoudinge, dit vra hy vir my
en vir jou. Verhoudinge met
ons broer en suster. Ek het
nie 'n suster nie. het net
vir Josh. het Jesus vir jou
ook gevra om vir hom te
leef en altyd huis beheer
vir hom, te vra. Eer God
hy vra eer hom van gesinne
hulle vrees hom nie.

But if anyone does not provide for his own, and especially for those of his household, he has denied the faith and is worse than an unbeliever.
I Timothy 5:8

dood wil
huil vir ons gee. Laat ek
vir jou iets vertel, dood sit
vir almal en wag. huil is nie
wat waarlik gebeur in
hemel hie. Daar sing almal
van vreugde. Wysheid sê
huil het hy vir ons gegee
om al van ons seer uit
te kry. Jesus vra vir
ons om huil vir hom te
gee. trane vang hy alles
op in die hemel vir almal.

Death wants to make us cry.
Let me tell you something: death waits for all of us.
In heaven there is no crying – everybody there sings joyfully!
Wisdom says that He has allowed tears in our lives
to get rid of some of the pain we have in our hearts.
Jesus asks us to give our crying to Him.
He catches all our tears and saves it in heaven.

"For the Lamb who is in the midst of the throne will shepherd them
and lead them to living fountains of waters.
And God will wipe away every tear from their eyes."
Revelation 7:17

hy sê liefde sal van hom af kom. Wou jy vir hom ook liefhê en jy weet nie hoe nie? Jesus is liefde al wat jy hoef te doen om vir hom te wys hoe lief jy hom het is vir dood gereed te wees elke dag. Dit deur werklik jou lewe vir hom te gee. God se liefde vir hom begin met nou verhouding met hom. Hy is lief vir jou, en vir my.

He says love comes from Him. Do you also want to love Him but you just don't know how? Jesus is love. All that you have to do to show Him how much you love Him is to live your life so that you will be ready for death every day. You can only do that by truly giving your life to Him. To love God starts by having an intimate relationship with Him. He loves you, and He loves me too.

17

There is no fear in love; but perfect love casts out fear,
because fear involves torment. But he who fears has not been made
perfect in love. We love Him because He first loved us.
1 John 4: 18-19

Wysheid seën jou, hy seën.
het jy nuwe hoop nodig?
hy is die hoop wat ons nodig
het. Jy sal sien wat sal
gebeur as jy hoop vir iets
kort, vra dan van hom want
hy is hoop. Ja seën is hoop
hoop is van Jesus, in hom
is alles wat jy nodig het.
Wysheid sê hy sal vir jou
vir altyd hoop hê. Jy hou
hoop vas, bid net en bly
vertrou dit is hoop. bid
is hoop, hoop is bid. God
is liefde.

Wisdom blesses you – He blesses you! Do you need new hope?
He is the hope that we need. You will see what will happen
when you start hoping. When you need something, ask Him for it –
because He is hope. Yes, to bless is to hope, and hope comes from
Jesus. In Him you will find everything you need.
Wisdom says that He will always have hope for you.
Hold on to your hope. Just pray, and keep on
trusting God – that is what it means to hope.
To pray is to hope, and to hope is to pray.
God is love.

I LOVE you!

And not only that, but we also glory in tribulations, knowing that tribulation produces perseverance; and perseverance, character; and character, hope. Now hope does not disappoint, because the love of God has been poured out in our hearts by the Holy Spirit who was given to us.
Romans 5:3-5

Wysheid sê hy wat homself
liewer het as vir Wysheid
is 'n fool. Want hy sê geseënd
is jy wat nie jouself liewer
het as God se woord nie.
Wysheid se bruid van Christus
sal haar lewe gee vir hom.
Wysheid sê, vat wat hy vir
mense gee, sal hy, vra om
ander mee te dien.

Wisdom says that he who loves himself more than he loves
Wisdom is a fool. He says:
"Blessed is he who doesn't love himself more than God's Word."
Wisdom says that the Bride of Christ will lay down her life for Him.
Wisdom says that He will ask you to serve
other people with the things that He gives you.

I have been crucified with Christ; it is no longer I who live,
but Christ lives in me; and the life which I now live in the flesh
I live by faith in the Son of God, who loved me and gave Himself for me.
Galatians 2:20

Wysheid sê nou is die tyd om nie liefde vir geld te hê nie, maar God bo alles. Wat vyand wil hê is dat mense besig moet raak met die wêreld en vergeet van God se Woord. Jesus staan en klop, hy wag om in te kom in jou lewe. hoekom wil jy nie oopmaak nie? Sal hy geloof in jou kry? my hart is so seer want hy sê. hy sal nie inkom as jy nie self oopmaak nie. Staan Jesus buite jou hart of binne?

Wisdom says that now is not the time to love money, but now we must love God above all! The enemy wants people to be busy with the things of the world and to forget about the Word of God. Jesus is knocking on our hearts. He is waiting to come into your life. Why don't you want to open the door for Him? Will He find faith in you? My heart is hurting because He says that He can't come in unless you open the door for Him.
Is Jesus standing outside your heart, or inside?

Behold, I stand at the door and knock.
If anyone hears My voice and opens the door,
I will come in to him and dine with him, and he with Me.
Revelation 3:20

Wysheid sê nou is wysheid
vir jou ook, Wag nie vir
wanneer jy nie meer kan
nie. Vra nou vir Jesus sy
Wysheid. God sê hy sal
vir jou lei tree vir tree.

Wisdom says that wisdom is now available for you too.
Don't wait until it is too late – ask Jesus right now for His wisdom.
God says He will lead you step by step.

Wisdom calls aloud outside; she raises her voice in the open squares.
She cries out in the chief concourses, at the openings of the gates
in the city. She speaks her words: "How long, you simple ones,
will you love simplicity? For scorners delight in their scorning,
and fools hate knowledge. Turn at my rebuke; surely I will
pour out my spirit on you; I will make my words known to you."
Proverbs 1:20-23

Wysheid sê: haat sal jy
moet neerlê en vergifnis
vra. Liefde is hoe ons
vrede kry in ons lewe
en harte. Weet jy daar
is vrede en liefde in
god, hy voed ons gees
deur sy Woord.

Wisdom says: "You have to lay down hatred
and ask for forgiveness."
Only through love can you receive peace in your life and heart.
Do you know that there is peace and love in God?
He feeds our spirit through His Word.

Therefore, as the elect of God, holy and beloved, put on tender mercies,
kindness, humility, meekness, longsuffering; bearing with one another,
and forgiving one another, if anyone has a complaint against another;
even as Christ forgave you, so you also must do.
But above all these things put on love, which is the bond of perfection.
And let the peace of God rule in your hearts,
to which also you were called in one body; and be thankful.
Colossians 3: 12-15

Wysheid is vir tieners
baie lief, hy wag vir
tieners om tyd met hom
te spandeer. Sal behoorlik
besef hoe nodig jy God
het wanneer niemand nou
by jou is nie en niemand
vir jou omgee nie. Dan weet
jy God sal jou nooit begewe en
jou nooit verlaat nie, nooit nie!

Wisdom loves teenagers very much.
He is waiting for teenagers to spend time with Him.
You will only realize how much you need God
when nobody is with you
and when nobody cares for you— then you will know that God
will never leave you nor forsake you.
No, never!

You're My
friend!

Let your conduct be without covetousness;
be content with such things as you have.
For He Himself has said, "I will never leave you nor forsake you."
So we may boldly say: "The LORD is my helper; I will not fear.
What can man do to me?"
Hebrews 13:5-6

Wysheid sê tieners rook
baie keer want hulle wil
so graag aanvaar word in
die wêreld. Hy sê rook
maak jou nie aanvaarbaar
nie vir jou om by mense
aanvaar te word moet jy
gelukkig met jouself wees
hy sê vir jou in hom
is vir jou vrede en geluk
vir jou en my sê hy my
kinders moenie rook nie
hou jou skoon en rein.
Satan wil jou afhanklik
maak rook is oorspronklik
vir mense om vas te raak
aan verslawing. Jesus wil
jou vrymaak. vra hom asb.

Wisdom says that many times teenagers start smoking
because they want to be accepted by the world.
He says that smoking won't make you popular.
In order for you to be accepted by people around you, you first have
to accept yourself. He says that true peace and happiness are
only found in Him. He says to you and me:
"My children, don't smoke. Keep yourself clean
and pure. Satan wants to bring you into bondage. The purpose
of smoking is to bring people into the bondage of addiction."
Jesus wants to set you free – please ask Him to do it.

24

Therefore do not let sin reign in your mortal body,
that you should obey it in its lusts. And do not present your members as
instruments of unrighteousness to sin, but present yourselves to God as
being alive from the dead, and your members as instruments
of righteousness to God. For sin shall not have dominion over you,
for you are not under law but under grace.
Romans 6: 13-14

Wysheid is hewige hewige bevryding. In hom is bevryding. Baie kinders is so vas vas vas! Satan hou hulle vas, hy wil nie hê kinders moet vry wees nie. Sal jy asb vir Jesus vra om jou vry te maak, as jy stemme hoor in jou kop wat jou sleg sê is dit satan. hy wou vir my ook sies sê, toe die hel wou hy my doodmaak Jesus het my toe gered met sy bloed.

Wisdom is your great, great deliverance!
In Him is freedom and deliverance.
So many children are bound by the enemy. It is Satan who is holding them in bondage because He doesn't want them to be free. Will you please ask Jesus to set you free? When you hear voices in your head telling you bad things about yourself, you can know that it is Satan telling you those things. He also wanted to tell me to be ashamed when the forces of hell tried to kill me. Jesus then saved me with His blood.

25

For though we walk in the flesh, we do not war according to the flesh.
For the weapons of our warfare are not carnal but mighty in God for
pulling down strongholds, casting down arguments and every high thing
that exalts itself against the knowledge of God, bringing every thought
into captivity to the obedience of Christ, and being ready to punish all
disobedience when your obedience is fulfilled.
2 Corinthians 10: 3-6

Wysheid sê beweeg in die
teenwoordigheid van God en
bly daar asb. by Wysheid
is alles wat jou sal gelukkig
maak. Vergeet wat verby is
en strek jou uit na wat voor
is. Wysheid sê voor lê jou
toekoms, sy liefde vir jou sal
lei. Weet jy ek was baie bang
oor my toekoms, toe wys
Wysheid sê toe Aldo, ek is
in beheer van jou lewe.
Weet jy vandag wens ek, ek
het nooit so getwyfel in god
nie. Hy is getrou.

Wisdom says that we need to move into the presence of God,
and that we must please stay there. In Wisdom you will find
everything you need for happiness. Forget what is behind you
and stretch yourself toward what lies ahead. Wisdom says that
your future lies ahead of you and that His love for you will lead you.
Did you know that I was very scared of what my
future would hold? Then Wisdom showed me
that He is in control of my life.
Today I wish that I never doubted in God – not even for a second.
He is so faithful.

26

Brethren, I do not count myself to have apprehended;
but one thing I do, forgetting those things which are behind
and reaching forward to those things which are ahead,
I press toward the goal for the prize
of the upward call of God in Christ Jesus.
Philippians 3: 13-14

Wysheid sê seuns en dogters vuur sien ek in joa skoot as jy rondslaap. Wysheid sê vir jou hoa jou reinig en heilig vir God. Jy soek net liefde van vriende en aanvaarding, dit kom deur jouself lief te hê en jou te aanvaar soos jy is, Sy liefde vir jou is groter as wat jy kan beleef deur sex. Seuns moenie, asb moenie begin eers dink nie bid eerder.

Wisdom says: "My sons and daughters, you take fire into your belly when you sleep around. Keep yourself pure and holy for God. You are only seeking love and acceptance from your friends, but it will come when you learn to love yourself and to accept yourself just the way you are." God's love for you is much greater than what you will ever experience through sex. Boys, please don't even start thinking about sex – rather pray.

27

Flee sexual immorality. Every sin that a man does is outside the body,
but he who commits sexual immorality sins against his own body.
Or do you not know that your body is the temple of the Holy Spirit
who is in you, whom you have from God, and you are not your own?
For you were bought at a price;
therefore glorify God in your body and in your spirit, which are God's.
I Corinthians 6:18-20

Wysheid sê suur wat vyand
op ons gooi is vloeke.
Jesus sê Jy het krag om
vloeke te breek. Jesus sê
woorde van dood is suur
wat vyand ons mee veg.
Wysheid sê moenie dat jou
woorde iemand se lewe
veg nie. Spreek woorde van
lewe oor almal. Jou mond
hou soveel krag vra wysheid
vir woorde.

Wisdom says that the acid the enemy is throwing on us is curses.
Jesus says you have the power to break the work of the curses.
Jesus says that the acid the enemy is using to fight us with
is the words of death people say about us.
Wisdom says that you mustn't let your words
be hurtful to any other person.
Speak words of life about everyone.
Your mouth holds so much power.
Ask Wisdom for the right words.

28

A man's stomach shall be satisfied from the fruit of his mouth;
from the produce of his lips he shall be filled.
Death and life are in the power of the tongue,
and those who love it will eat its fruit.
Proverbs 18:20-21

Wysheid sê hoe sal jy kan
leef sonder geloof? Geloof
moet gedryf word deur liefde
Liefde is so deel van geloof
Sal jy vir hom vertel hoe
lief jy hom het? Want sonder
liefde sal jy nie kan lewe
nie. Lou christene het nie
geloof nie, hulle glo in hulle
eie krag. Asb moenie sonder
geloof leef nie, veg die goeie
geveg van geloof. Wysheid
sê hy sal jou vat na
vryheid, sal jy net glo Hy
is God!

Wisdom asks: "How do you think you will be able to live without faith?"
Faith needs to be driven forward by love. Love is a part of faith.
Will you tell Him how much you love Him?
Because you won't be able to live without love.
Luke-warm Christians don't have faith –
they trust in their own abilities.
Please, don't live without faith.
Fight the good fight of faith.
Wisdom says that He will lead you to freedom
if you only believe that He is truly God!

29

But without faith it is impossible to please Him,
for he who comes to God must believe that He is,
and that He is a rewarder of those who diligently seek Him.
Hebrews 11:6

Wysheid sê vir jou hier is nuwe wyn by hom. ek sê vir jou nuwe wyn is sy groot liefde in sy woord, sy anointing. Wyn van die wêreld is vir tieners net 'n manier wat hulle wil groot lyk. Sal jy asb hoor wat Wysheid sê, jou sien hy reeds volwasse deur sy oë, moenie drank drink om groot te wil lyk nie. Deur sy oë lyk dit foolish.

Wisdom says that He has "new wine" for us to drink.
I am telling you that this "new wine" is God's amazing love
that He reveals to us through His Word.
It is His anointing.
Teenagers use the "wine of the world" as a way
to make them feel better about themselves.
Will you please listen to what Wisdom has to say?
He says that in His eyes you are already mature;
you don't need wine to be accepted by others.
In His eyes that is foolishness.

30

See then that you walk circumspectly, not as fools but as wise,
redeeming the time, because the days are evil. Therefore
do not be unwise, but understand what the will of the Lord is. And do not
be drunk with wine, in which is dissipation; but be filled with the Spirit.
Ephesians 5: 15-18

You're My Friend!

Wysheid sê help is net by hom. hier op aarde roep almal na hulp maar hy is die enigste hulp. hy was vir my by hewige geveg vir my lewe, my enigste hulp. Sy bloed was wat my gered het. die vyand wou dir my beveg toe roep ek na God — sy Woord is lewend, Wanneer ek dit eet raak ek vol van Sy waarhede seën is in God, bly in hom, roep net na hom, ek seën jou vandag, verseën is jy.

Wisdom says that only He is our helper. Here on earth everyone calls out for help, but He is our only helper. When I was fighting the greatest battle of my life I could only trust in Him for help. It was His blood (the blood of Jesus) that saved me. The enemy tried to overcome me, but then I called out to God.
His Word is living! When I ate His Word I became full of His truth.
True blessing is found in God. Stay in Him and call out to Him.
I bless you today – blessed are you!

31

"If you love Me, keep My commandments. And I will pray the Father,
and He will give you another Helper, that He may abide with you forever
— the Spirit of truth, whom the world
cannot receive, because it neither sees Him nor knows Him;
but you know Him, for He dwells with you and will be in you.
I will not leave you orphans; I will come to you."
John 14: 15-18

Wysheid sê: God, sy huis, sy
regte liefde vir ons, seën
ons. Wysheid sê vir elkeen
wat hom soek, sal hom vind.
Gaan op jou kniee so sal jy
verseker verseker hom vind.
hy het vir my uit 'n gat
van dood gehaal net omdat
ek na hom geroep het. Sal
jy my glo Jesus sê ons is
vir hom so spesiaal hy het
sy lewe gegee vir ons. God
sê hy sal jou weer lewe
gee, hy gee lewe aan die
wat geloof in hom het. Gister
nadat ek almal in my skool
se voete gewas het, het Jesus
vir my gewys hoe ek by 'n
venster uitvlieg op sy vlerke
hy sê toe: Aldo vlieg, by my
is vlerke, by my is wat jy
nodig het. hy sê: Jy is gereed
nou om vir my te werk. Wie
haat het is verlore.

Wisdom says:"God, His house, and His pure love for us, is the true blessing."
Wisdom says that everyone who seeks Him will find Him.
Go down on your knees – that way you will definitely find Him! He pulled me
out of a deep dark pit of death because I called to Him to save me.
Will you please believe me when I tell you that Jesus says we are so special
to Him? He gave His life for us. God says He will give
you life again – He gives life to those who believe in Him.
Yesterday, after I washed all of my classmates' feet,
Jesus showed me in a vision how I flew out of the window on His wings.
He then said to me: "Aldo, keep on flying! I am your wings.
I have everything you need. You are now ready to work for me."
Those who have hatred in them are lost.

for You

For I know the thoughts that I think toward you, says the LORD,
thoughts of peace and not of evil, to give you a future and a hope.
Then you will call upon Me and go and pray to Me, and I will listen to you.
And you will seek Me and find Me,
when you search for Me with all your heart.
Jeremiah 29: 11-13

Wysheid sê hou vas aan sy belofte
hy is wie hy sê hy is. Wie
in sy Woord glo sal sien hoe
jou lewe sal verander. hy het
Heilige Gees vir ons gegee om ons
te help sy Woord is lewe. Sy
Gees is in ons.

Wisdom says that we have to hold on to His promise.
He is who He says He is!
Those who believe in Him
will see how their lives will be transformed.
He gave us His Holy Spirit to help us.
His Word is life and His Spirit lives in us.

33

It is the Spirit who gives life; the flesh profits nothing.
The words that I speak to you are spirit, and they are life.
John 6:63

Wysheid sê hy sal tieners sy
hart wys, baie sal sien seer
in hulle lewe is UTF verander
toe verander van my seer
na God se hart vir my
lewe. hier is hewige wreed
vyand wat jou hart so seer
wil maak. Gesien hoe hy
vir tieners baie haat, gaan
na jou Abba Vader en wys
hom jou seer hart hy
vuur vir ons teen satan.
Sal jy vir hom vertrou
met jou hart asb?

Wisdom says that He will reveal His heart to teenagers, and many of
these teenagers will then realize that He has transformed the pain
in their lives. He took my pain and He changed it so that I reflected
more of God's heart through my life.
There is a cruel enemy out there who wants to cause a lot of pain
in our lives (Satan).
I saw that he really hates teenagers.
Go to your Abba Father and show Him your hurting
heart. He will be a fire of protection for us against Satan.
Will you please trust Him with your whole heart?

34

Search me, O God, and know my heart; try me, and know my anxieties;
and see if there is any wicked way in me,
and lead me in the way everlasting.
Psalm 139:23-24

Wysheid sê vuur sal hy by
vurige hart wat gebreek is.
gee. Jy is vir Jesus so baie
belangrik. hy sal so vir jou
van homself leer. het vir
humble kind van God vreeslik
humble hart gegee. Jy moet
net jou lewe neerlê vir
Jesus. Wysheid sê hy haat
vreeslik mense wat dink hulle
is beter as ander. hy vra
'n nederige hart. giet in
vuur hulle wat trotse bome
is, vol pride. Vir Jesus se koning
kryk is humble hart nodig.

Wisdom says that He will give His (holy) fire to the brokenhearted.
You are so important to Jesus. He will teach you about Himself.
He will give His children humble hearts when they lay down their lives
for Jesus. Wisdom says that He really hates it when people think they
are better than others.
He is seeking a humble heart.
He will pour out His fire on those
who stand tall and prideful as trees.
For Jesus' Kingdom we need humble hearts.

35

But he who is greatest among you shall be your servant.
And whoever exalts himself will be humbled,
and he who humbles himself will be exalted.
Matthew 23: 11-12

Wysheid sê: hy is huis, huis
vir verlore siele. Wysheid
vuur sy liefde is so groot
hy vuur nuwe liefde vir almal
wat hom aaneem. hy het vir
jou gesterf aan die kruis
vir jou het hy nuwe lewe
in hom, rat net alles. geseënd
is jy wat hom vertrou
vandag wanneer jy 'n keuse
maak, nou sal jy voel hoe
hy jou hart aanraak.
hy verlang na ons tieners
ook, vir altyd sal hy na jou kyk.

Wisdom says that He is a home to lost souls. Wisdom says that the fire
of His love is so big that He has enough love to give to everybody
who accepts Him. He (Jesus) died for you on the cross,
and He came to give you new life that is only found in Him –
all we have to do is to receive it all!
Blessed are you when you trust Him
in all your choices –
you will experience how He touches your heart.
He longs for the teenagers to turn to Him.
He will look after us forever.

36

Blessed be the God and Father of our Lord Jesus Christ,
who has blessed us with every spiritual blessing in the heavenly places
in Christ, just as He chose us in Him before the foundation of the world,
that we should be holy and without blame before Him in love,
having predestined us to adoption as sons by Jesus Christ to Himself,
according to the good pleasure of His will, to the praise of the glory
of His grace, by which He made us accepted in the Beloved.
Ephesians 1: 3-6

Wysheid sê verloor jou lewe
sodat hy jou sy lewe kan gee.
haat het hy vir my gewys
kom uit die hel uit. Jesus is
verhoudinge se antwoord. Jy sal
vrede maak en in liefde beleef
hoe hy vir jou veg. Gaan en
wees net die minste nou.
Wysheid vra vir tieners of
hy oor verlede kan bloed,
sy bloed, kan gooi sodat verlede
uitgewis kan word. hoeveel
van ons vra vir God vir 'n
lewe van oorvloed. hy sê
lê net jou lewe neer vir my.

Wisdom says: "Lose your life in order that He (Christ) can give you His life." He showed me that hatred comes from hell. Jesus is the answer to all your relationship problems. You will make peace and experience love. You will also see how He fights your battles for you. Go, and choose to be the least. Wisdom is asking the teens if they will allow Him to pour out His blood (the blood of Jesus) on their past so that it can be wiped clean and redeemed. There are so many of us who ask God for a life of abundance, but He says that all we need to do in order to receive it is to lay down our lives for Him.

37

Then Jesus said to His disciples, "If anyone desires to come after Me,
let him deny himself, and take up his cross, and follow Me.
For whoever desires to save his life will lose it, but whoever loses his life
for My sake will find it. For what profit is it to a man if he gains the whole
world, and loses his own soul? Or what will a man give in exchange for his
soul? For the Son of Man will come in the glory of His Father
with His angels, and then He will reward each according to his works.
Matthew 16:24-27

Wysheid sê: tieners in God
is hoop vir jou, vat sy
raad wat in die Woord van
God is vir jou. Sy raad
is hulp vir almal wat
moedeloos is. hulp, vuur al
die vurige pyle van die vyand
af. hy het self vir my,
vir elke hewige aanval van
vyand hulp gegee deur
Sy Woord. ek lees elke
vry oomblik sy Woord want
hy lewe! Vat sy Woord
en lees dit. help is hier
in Sy Woord.

Wisdom says: "Teenagers, in God there is hope for you."
Keep the instructions He gives you in the Word of God.
His advice will help anyone who is feeling hopeless.
Hope is the fire of God that will protect you
from all the fiery arrows of the enemy.
I can testify that in every attack of the enemy
I faced, He helped me with His Word.
I read the Word every spare moment I can get because He lives!
Take His Word and read it. You will find the help you need in His Word.

38

How can a young man cleanse his way?
By taking heed according to Your word.
With my whole heart I have sought You; Oh, let me not wander
from Your commandments! Your word I have hidden in my heart,
that I might not sin against You.
Psalm 119:9-11

Wysheid sê sal jy hart van klip vir vryheid in Hom verruil? Ja, vryheid is so nuut vir my. met vuur van god en Jesus se bloed het ek vry gekom. Harde hart van oupa het haat gehou teen swart mense. So vuur harde vuur toe vir my deur 'n bloedlyn vloek. Oupa het vergifnis aan Jesus gevra en ek het vry gekom. Wysheid sê ons mag geen haat in harte hê nie dit gee harde harte.

Wisdom says: "Will you exchange your heart of stone for freedom in Him?' Yes, I received freedom through the blood of Jesus and the fire of God. My grandfather's hardened heart held hatred against people. His hardened heart was a channel through which the enemy could send "fire" to attack me because of the bloodline curse. My grandpa repented and asked Jesus to forgive him, and therefore I was set free from the curse of hatred.
Wisdom says we are not allowed to have any hatred in our hearts – it will lead to hardened hearts.

39

I will give you a new heart and put a new spirit within you;
I will take the heart of stone out of your flesh
and give you a heart of flesh.
I will put My Spirit within you and cause you to walk in My statutes,
and you will keep My judgments and do them.
Then you shall dwell in the land that I gave to your fathers;
you shall be My people, and I will be your God.
Ezekiel 36:26-28

Wysheid sê tieners sal
vrae vanself wil antwoord
maar hy sê hy is die
antwoord op al jou vrae.
Hy sê gaan op jou kniee
en vra hom wat jy wil
weet, sy Heilige Gees sal
vir jou wat vra antwoord.
Wysheid is so hewige vuur
wat antwoord. hy is
haar fyn hy het jou
lewe haarfyn beplan so
vra maar jou vrae vir God.

Wisdom says that teenagers cry a lot because of their parents
arguments, and that the enemy uses this pain as fire against them.
Wisdom says to teenagers that they should take all their pain to God.
He is the one who will comfort you.
Pray for your parents – give them to Jesus.
You must bless them. Ask Wisdom to teach you
if you don't know how – He will help you.
There is tremendous power in blessing someone else.
Please; help your parents and bless them with God's love.

40

However, when He, the Spirit of truth, has come,
He will guide you into all truth; for He will not speak on His own authority,
but whatever He hears He will speak; and He will tell you things to come.
John 16: 13

Wysheid sal vir ons tieners
vuur van God gee want
ons is nuwe generasie
tieners. Hy sê Joel 2
kinders is vuur van God
tieners. Hy rig 'n weermag
op in die gees. Hy sê ek
vuur vuur sit hy op rooi
bloed gewaste bloed van
Jesus gewaste tieners. Jy
huil oor seer in jou hart
bloed van Jesus is wat
harte skoon was en genees.
Hy het vir my 'n nuwe hart
wat rooi skoon is gegee. Nou
is ek so baie gelukkig. regtig
waar gelukkig.

Wisdom will give us teens the fire of God, because we are a new generation teenagers! He says that Joel 2 children are the "fire of God" children. He is busy raising up an army in the spirit. He says that He will place His holy fire on the teens that have been washed clean by the blood of Jesus. Are you crying because of all the pain in your heart? The blood of Jesus will wash your heart clean and heal the pain. He gave me a new heart that is red (covered by Jesus' blood) and pure. Now I am so happy! I am really, really happy!

41

"And it shall come to pass afterward that I will pour out My Spirit
on all flesh; your sons and your daughters shall prophesy,
your old men shall dream dreams,
your young men shall see visions. And also on My menservants
and on My maidservants I will pour out My Spirit in those days."
Joel 2:28-29

Wysheid sê wat tieners vuur is
huil oor hewige baie baie helse
baklei van ouers. Wysheid sê
vir tieners vat al jou seer
na God toe. Hy is wie vir
jou wil troos. het vir ouers
vuur gebede - gee hulle vir
Jesus. Jy seën hulle, vra
vir Wysheid, hy sal jou help.
Seën het baie krag, asb help
jou ouers en seën hulle met
God se liefde.

Wisdom says the arguments of their parents cause teenagers
a lot of pain and tears, and that the enemy uses this pain as (enemy)
fire* against them.
Wisdom says to teenagers that they should take all their pain to God.
He is the one who will comfort you.
Pray for your parents – give them to Jesus.
You must bless them. If you don't know how;
ask Wisdom to teach you – He will help you.
There is tremendous power in blessing someone else.
Please; help your parents and bless them with God's love.

*enemy fire =
A term Aldo
uses when he refers
to the arrows of "fire"
sent by the evil one
to attack us.

42

Blessed be the God and Father of our Lord Jesus Christ,
the Father of mercies and God of all comfort,
who comforts us in all our tribulation, that we may be able to comfort
those who are in any trouble, with the comfort
with which we ourselves are comforted by God.
2 Corinthians 1: 3-4

Wysheid sê: Vat help vir julle
wat hulp van hom vra die
hulp is van ons Vader
wat hemel en aarde gemaak
het. dan Gaat vyand dit
hy wil hê ons moet self
regkom sodat hy ons kan
moedeloos maak. hulp is
van God hy wil hê ons moet
so afhanklik van hom wees.
Sal jy van nou af voor
jy 'n besluit maak dit vir
God gee- die tou doring
in vlees is ons eie ek...
Vat vooropgestelde idees
na God toe.

Wisdom says: "To those who seek help from God,
their help will come from our Father who created heaven and earth."
The enemy hates it when this happens.
He wants us to try and fix things by ourselves;
that way he can cause us to become discouraged.
Our help is from God! He wants us to be totally
dependent on Him. Will you seek God's will
before you make a decision,
and hand everything over to Him from now on?
The thorn in our flesh is the "selfish-I" that we have to die to.
Take your preconceived ideas to God.

43

I will lift up my eyes to the hills — From whence comes my help?
My help comes from the LORD, Who made heaven and earth.
Psalm 121: 1-2

Wysheid sê ouers sien dat
hulle tieners vuur soek.
Hy sê vir ouers vat ook
jouself na waar god se
Gees is. die gees van
God is wat tieners soek
na rooi die bloed v. d Lam
hy is al wat ons
nodig het. Want die dou
liefde van God bring lewe.
daar is geen liefde wat
by God se riefde kom nie

Wisdom says that parents can see that their teenagers
are seeking for more fire from God (to live their lives 'on fire' for Him).
He says that our parents should also give themselves
to God in order to be led by the Spirit of God.
Teenagers are looking
for the red blood of the Lamb.
He (Jesus) is all that we need;
because the dew-love* of God brings life.
No other love will ever be able to compare to God's love.

*dew-love =
the
unconditional
love of God

44

I love you!

I sleep, but my heart is awake; it is the voice of my beloved!
He knocks, saying, "Open for me, my sister,
my love, My dove, my perfect one;
For my head is covered with dew,
My locks with the drops of the night."
Song of Songs 5:2

Wysheid sê nou is tyd
wat seën sal uitgestort
word hy vat huil en
verander na seën. Wysheid
het vir my vertel
hy vat huil en sit
seën daarop. daar is
Seën op ons, want vyand
hy wou van ons huil
huil toe vat God dit
vuur en verander hy
dit na seën. ons is so
Wysheid so geseënd baie
dankie Jesus. Hy is my
redder en Koning.

Wisdom says that now is the time when He will pour out His blessing.
He will take all the tears we have cried
and He will change them into blessings.
Wisdom told me that he takes our tears
and He puts His blessing on it.
God's blessing is upon us.
The enemy wanted to make us cry many tears,
but God took the enemy's fire and He transformed
into blessings. We are so blessed by Wisdom.
Thank You Jesus! He is my Savior and my King.

Now I saw heaven opened, and behold, a white horse.
And He who sat on him was called Faithful and True,
and in righteousness He judges and makes war.
His eyes were like a flame of fire, and on His head were many crowns.
He had a name written that no one knew except Himself.
He was clothed with a robe dipped in blood,
and His name is called The Word of God.
Revelation 19: 11-13

Wysheid sê hy is wie die
hoop is vir die wêreld.
Jy is wys as wysheid van
God vir jou weg aanwys.
Sal jy vir hom vat al jou
nou seer jou ou seer, ook
seer wat jy nie baie wil
oor praat nie. Wie is
wys, hy wie van God eet
en van hom drink.
Wysheid sê hy is die
bron van lewe.

Wisdom says that He is the hope of the world.
You are wise when you follow in the way that Wisdom leads you.
Will you take all your pain to Him?
The pain you are experiencing now,
the pain you still have from the past,
and the pain that you don't want to talk about.
Who is wise?
He who eats and drinks from God.
Wisdom says that He is the source of life.

Jesus answered, "Everyone who drinks this water will be thirsty again,
but whoever drinks the water I give them will never thirst.
Indeed, the water I give them will become in them
a spring of water welling up to eternal life."
John 4: 13-14

Wysheid sê vroom so vroom
voor ouers maar hoekom
so voorbarig en hart met
jou vriende. Wat as jy
besef ek woon in jou hart
en ek sien hoe jy 'n
dubbel lewe leef. hou vas
aan die waarheid van my
Woord. hou jou hart rein
van boosheid. Saai waarheid
en jy sal baie lewe maai.
Wysheid sê so sal jy
van waarheid Lewe en gelukkig
wees.

Wisdom says: "Why are you so pious before your parents, but so arrogant and loud before your friends? What will you do when you realize that I live in your heart and I can see that you are living a life of double-standards?
Hold on to the truth of My Word.
Keep your heart pure from evil.
Sow truth and you will reap life."
Wisdom says that by doing this you will live your life in truth and you will be happy.

Do not be deceived, God is not mocked;
for whatever a man sows, that he will also reap.
For he who sows to his flesh will of the flesh reap corruption,
but he who sows to the Spirit will of the Spirit reap everlasting life.
Galatians 6:7-8

Wysheid sê sy hart vir
tieners is om seer te
kry nie. Hy sê gee jou
hart vir my. nou sal ek
jou beskerm teen die vyand
se werke. Jesus is wat jy
nodig het, sal jy my glo
vandag asb. ek self het
ook seer gekry toe ek my
oë van Jesus afgehaal het
vir 'n sekere tgd in my lewe
Hy het vir my kom haal
daar diep in 'n gat toe
ek na hom geroep het.
roep na Jesus hy sal jou
red.

Wisdom says that it is His heart's desire that teens don't get hurt.
He says: "Give your heart to Me.
Now I will protect you from the enemy and his works."
Jesus is the one you need. Will you please believe me today?
There was a time in my life when I took my eyes off
Jesus and I also got hurt.
He came and pulled me out
of that deep pit when I called out to Him.
Call out to Jesus, He will save you.

You're My Friend!

I waited patiently for the LORD; And He inclined to me, And heard my cry.
He also brought me up out of a horrible pit, Out of the miry clay,
And set my feet upon a rock, And established my steps.
He has put a new song in my mouth — Praise to our God;
Many will see it and fear, And will trust in the LORD.
Psalm 40: 1-3

Wysheid sê vir my hy soek
van tieners se lewe rein-
heid. God is heilig en hy
vra van ons leef heilig
vir hom. Jy sal van hom
eet, sy boom, dan sal jy
heilige vrugte dra. God
se troon is vol van sy
Glorie en die engele sing
heilig heilig heilig is die
Lam van God. ek het self
heilig heilig heilig gesing
voor sy troon. Hy vra
tieners sal jy nou heilig
wandel elke dag.

Wisdom told me that He wants teenagers to live pure lives.
God is holy, and He asks us to live holy lives for Him.
You will eat of Him (His tree) and then you will produce holy fruits.
God's throne is full of His glory and the angels sing
'Holy, Holy, Holy is the Lamb of God'.
I also sang 'Holy, Holy, Holy'
when I was before His throne.
He asks the teenagers:
"Will you live a holy life for Me every day?

for You

49

Before the throne there was a sea of glass, like crystal.
And in the midst of the throne, and around the throne,
were four living creatures full of eyes in front and in back.
The first living creature was like a lion, the second living creature
like a calf, the third living creature had a face like a man, and the fourth
living creature was like a flying eagle. The four living creatures,
each having six wings, were full of eyes around and within.
And they do not rest day or night, saying:
"Holy, holy, holy, Lord God Almighty, Who was and is and is to come!"
Revelation 4:6-8

Wysheid vat oornag al jou
vuur weg wat Lusifer jou
mee vuur wanneer jy dit
alles aan hom gee, jou
sondes erken belei en
laat staan. Jesus sal vir
jou ook vry maak vir ewig.
Hy sal jou nooit begewe
of verlaat nie. glo vir my
Hy sal altyd hoog jou optel.
Hy het vir my uit die dood
gered, vir ewig sal ek hom
eer. Ja, hy is wat sy Woord
sê getrou en nie 'n mens
dat hy kan lieg nie.

Wisdom will take away the evil fire
in the blink of an eye when you hand over everything to Him.
Acknowledge, repent, and turn away from your sins.
Jesus will set you free forever!
He will never leave you nor forsake you.
Believe me; He will always lift you up high,
He saved me from death and I will honor Him
forever. Yes, He is what His Word says He is: He is faithful.
He is not a man that He can lie.

_____

50

And I heard a loud voice from heaven saying,
"Behold, the tabernacle of God is with men, and He will dwell with
them, and they shall be His people. God Himself will be with them
and be their God.
And God will wipe away every tear from their eyes; there shall be no
more death, nor sorrow, nor crying. There shall be no more pain,
for the former things have passed away."
Then He who sat on the throne said, "Behold, I make all things new."
And He said to me, "Write, for these words are true and faithful."
Revelation 21: 3-5

Wysheid sê so baie het hy
jou lief dat sy eie seun,
hy Jesus, hy het sy
lewe vir jou gegee sodat
jy en ek vir ewig
Hom hart en siel
kan liefhê en deur hom
leef. Hy is Almagtig
waardig so waardig.
hoeveel is hy 'n werklikhêd
glo vir my my lewe
hy sal jou ewige lewe gee.
hy wat opgestaan het seën
jou as sy bruid.

Wisdom says that He loves you so much that He gave His only Son
Jesus for you. Jesus gave His life for us so that you and I will love Him
forever with our whole heart and soul, and so that we can live
forever through Him.
He is almighty, and so worthy of our praise.
He truly exists.
Believe me, Jesus will give you eternal life.
The One that rose from the dead (Jesus Christ)
blesses you as His Bride.

I LOVE You!

Then one of them, a lawyer, asked Him a question, testing Him,
and saying, "Teacher, which is the great commandment in the law?"
Jesus said to him, "'You shall love the LORD your God with all your heart,
with all your soul, and with all your mind.'
This is the first and great commandment.
And the second is like it: 'You shall love your neighbor as yourself.'
On these two commandments hang all the Law and the Prophets."
Matthew 22:35-40

Wysheid sê sy woord is
wat jou moet lei soos 'n
lamp in donker dae. dou
liefde is sy liefde so
Lewe is sy lig en so
gee sy lig Lewe en insig.
Wysheid sê sy lig is sy
waarheid sy en ek moet
in die lig van Jesus bly.
Wat jou so aanval is
uit duister sal jy in
die Lig bly asb. Jesus
is die lig van die wêreld

Wisdom says that His Word must be a lamp
that leads you through dark days.
His love is dew-love. His life is light,
and His light will give you life and insight.
Wisdom says His light is His truth.
You and I must live in Jesus' light.
The things that attack you come from darkness.
Will you please stay in the light?
Jesus is the light of the world.

52

This is the message which we have heard from Him and declare to you, that God is light and in Him is no darkness at all. If we say that we have fellowship with Him, and walk in darkness, we lie and do not practice the truth. But if we walk in the light as He is in the light, we have fellowship with one another, and the blood of Jesus Christ His Son cleanses us from all sin.
I John 1:5-7

Wysheid sê sy seun jou
liefde ware liefde is
wat Hy vir jou het.
Wat is hulle wat voor
God staan en God nie
vat nie, sy Lewe wil
neerlê vir God nie. Sal
jy baie vinnig asb God
alles gee wat jy het
harte van klip sal verander
soos jy alles vir God gee.
Wysheid sê sy seun Jesus
is waar lewe is lewe
is nie in jouself nie.

Wisdom says that His Son is dew-love – true love – and that is
what He wants to give to you. Who are they who stand before God
but don't want to receive Him? They are the ones who don't want to
lay down their lives for God. Please, don't waste time – give God your
entire life; give Him everything.
Hearts of stone will then be transformed
as you give everything to God.
Wisdom says that Jesus is true life.
Your life is not for yourself, but for God.

53

Beloved, let us love one another, for love is of God;
and everyone who loves is born of God and knows God.
He who does not love does not know God, for God is love.
In this the love of God was manifested toward us,
that God has sent His only begotten Son into the world,
that we might live through Him. In this is love, not that we loved God,
but that He loved us and sent His Son to be the propitiation for our sins.
Beloved, if God so loved us, we also ought to love one another.
I John 4: 7-11

Wysheid sê vir ons tieners
sal jy wat ek jou vra
doen. Jy is gevang, gevang
in 'n greep van leuns wat
Satan jou wil hou. Jesus
sê jy is so mooi net
soos jy is hy sê jy van
hou af moet jy in sy
oë kyk vir hoor hoe mooi
jy is en sien hoe jy lyk.
Stop! stop! hy satan wil vir
jou sê jy is te vet, te klein, te
swak, hy sien hy kan jou so
doodmaak. Wysheid sê jy is in
God se beeld gemaak. ek ook
ek sal nie meer na satan luister nie.

Wisdom says to us teens: "Will you do what I ask you to do?"
You have been caught up in the web of lies that Satan tried
to capture you with. Jesus says you are beautiful just the way you are.
Jesus says from now on you must look into His eyes to hear
how beautiful you are and to see what you truly look like.
Stop! Stop listening to Satan! He wants to tell you
that you are too fat, or too small or too weak...
He knows that he can kill you this way.
Wisdom says you were made in God's image.
I will also no longer listen to Satan's lies.

54

Be sober, be vigilant; because your adversary the devil
walks about like a roaring lion,
seeking whom he may devour. Resist him, steadfast in the faith,
knowing that the same sufferings
are experienced by your brotherhood in the world.
I Peter 5:8-9

Wysheid sê sy seuns is
'Sons of God'. Jy is nou
'n tiener maar God wil jou
'n seun van god maak. Seuns
is vir jou as 'n dogter ook.
Dit is 'n bewys van jou
grootword, volwasse word.
Jy is in god se oë 'n seun
Jy moet die dinge van 'n
kind neerlê jy moet begin
groei in Christus deur te
eet van Hom. Christus is
die boom van lewe. Wysheid
sê sy seuns sal lewe in
sy volheid.

Wisdom says that His sons are the sons of God.
You are a teenager now, but God wants to make you a son of God.
Girls are also sons of God.
When you are called a son of God it is proof that you have grown up
and are mature. In God's eyes you are a son.
You must lay down the childish things and you must
start growing in Christ by eating of Him.
Christ is the tree of life.
Wisdom says His sons will live in His fullness.

55

For as many as are led by the Spirit of God, these are sons of God.
For you did not receive the spirit of bondage again to fear,
but you received the Spirit of adoption by whom we cry out,
"Abba, Father." The Spirit Himself bears witness with our spirit
that we are children of God, and if children, then heirs —
heirs of God and joint heirs with Christ,
if indeed we suffer with Him, that we may also be glorified together.
Romans 8: 14-17

Wysheid sê jy vra hoe
sal ek een Word met u. Hy
sê soek my en jy sal my
vind. harde harte moet repent
harde harte is vrees harte.
Jesus het jou hart en jou
toekoms in Sy hande. Jy
moet oorgee aan hom.
Ek leef een tree op 'n slag
sal jy ook asb. Kies net
en sê , Jesus hier is my lewe
ek gee alles alles nou oor
aan u alleen. Ek is lief vir
u Jesus, God en Heilige gees.
Liefde Aldo mc Pherson.

Wisdom says that you are wondering how you can become one
with Him. He says that when you seek Him, you will find Him.
Hardened hearts must repent because hardened hearts are full of
fear. Jesus has your heart and your future in His hands.
You must give your life over to Him.
I live my life one step at a time.
Will you please do the same?
Just choose, and say to Jesus:
"Jesus here is my life. I hand everything over into Your hands –
to You and You alone. I love You so much Jesus!"

I love you Jesus,
God and Holy Spirit.
Love,
Aldo McPherson

My sheep hear My voice, and I know them, and they follow Me.
And I give them eternal life, and they shall never perish;
neither shall anyone snatch them out of My hand.
My Father, who has given them to Me, is greater than all;
and no one is able to snatch them out of My Father's hand.
I and My Father are one.
John 10:27-30

ALDO'S "LINGO"

Fire: A term Aldo uses when he refers to the arrows of "fire" sent by the evil one (Satan) to attack us (see James 3:5-6, and Psalm 5 7:4).

Drain: A gateway through which the evil one can operate. Like a sewerage drain, a "drain" in the spirit is a channel for dirt and filth to be transported and it can give demons access to our lives.

Drill: In Bible times the people built strong walls around the cities of Israel to protect the inhabitants. The Lord revealed to Aldo that like Nehemiah had to rebuild the walls of Jerusalem, so we also have to rebuild the walls of protection around our soul. The enemy will "drill" against our walls hoping to break down the wall and attack us through "soul wounds". (Read Nehemiah 1-7).

Red: When Aldo uses the word "red" he speaks of the blood of the Lamb – the blood of Jesus Christ. It refers to the redemptive power of the blood and the protection we have under the New Covenant (see Heb. 9:11-15).

Made in the USA
Columbia, SC
06 April 2023

14910432R00067